EDITORIAL

IN THIS ISSUE:

tourism TATTLER
ISSUE 04 APRIL 2016

PUBLISHER
Tourism Tattler (Pty) Ltd.
PO Box 891, Umhlanga Rocks, 4320
KwaZulu-Natal, South Africa.
Website: www.tourismtattler.com

EXECUTIVE EDITOR Des Langkilde
Cell: +27 (0)82 374 7260
Fax: +27 (0)86 651 8080
E-mail: editor@tourismtattler.com
Skype: tourismtattler

MAGAZINE ADVERTISING
ADVERTISING DIRECTOR Bev Langkilde
Cell: +27 (0)71 224 9971
Fax: +27 (0)86 656 3860
E-mail: bev@tourismtattler.com
Skype: bevtourismtattler

SUBSCRIPTIONS
http://eepurl.com/bocldD

BACK ISSUES (Click on the covers below).

CONTENTS

EDITORIAL
- **04** Accreditation
- **05** Cover Story

ATTRACTIONS
- **06 - 07** Explore Port Elizabeth
- **08 - 13** Where to Stay in and around Port Elizabeth
- **14 - 15** What to See and Do in and around Port Elizabeth

BUSINESS
- **18** SATSA Market Intelligence Report

COMPETITION
- **19** Win a Dietz Monarch D10 Hurricane Lantern

ENVIRONMENT
- **20** Conserving Energy, Reducing Waste

EVENTS
- **22 - 23** 2016 ASEAN Tourism Forum
- **24 - 25** Organic Food for Conscious Conferencing

HOSPITALITY
- **26 - 27** Property Profile: Travessia Beach Lodge
- **28 - 31** African Cuisine

LEGAL
- **32** The Consumer Protection Act - Part 3

MARKETING
- **33** Food in Tourism Marketing

RISK
- **34 - 35** Understanding Tourism Trade Insurance - Part 4

EDITORIAL CONTRIBUTORS
Adv. Louis Nel
Bennet Otoo
Des Langkilde
Dr. Peter E. Tarlow
Mandlakazi Skefile
Martin Janse van Vuuren
Tessa Buhrmann

MAGAZINE SPONSORS
- **03** The Mozambique Collection
- **16** Untouched Africa
- **16** Stormsriver Adventures
- **16** Kuzuko Lodge
- **17** The Hub Boutique Hotel
- **17** Cape Flame Guesthouse
- **17** Pine Lodge Resort
- **21** Inkwenkwezi Game Reserve
- **36** National Sea Rescue Institute

Disclaimer: The Tourism Tattler is published by Tourism Tattler (Pty) Ltd and is the official trade journal of the Southern Africa Tourism Services Association (SATSA). The Tourism Tattler digital e-zine is distributed free of charge to bona fide tourism stakeholders. Letters to the Editor are assumed intended for publication in whole or part and may therefore be used for such purpose. The information provided and opinions expressed in this publication are provided in good faith and do not necessarily represent the opinions of Tourism Tattler (Pty) Ltd, SATSA, its staff and its production suppliers. Advice provided herein should not be soley relied upon as each set of circumstances may differ. Professional advice should be sought in each instance. Neither Tourism Tattler (Pty) Ltd, SATSA, its staff and its production suppliers can be held legally liable in any way for damages of any kind whatsoever arising directly or indirectly from any facts or information provided or omitted in these pages or from any statements made or withheld or from supplied photographs or graphic images reproduced by the publication.

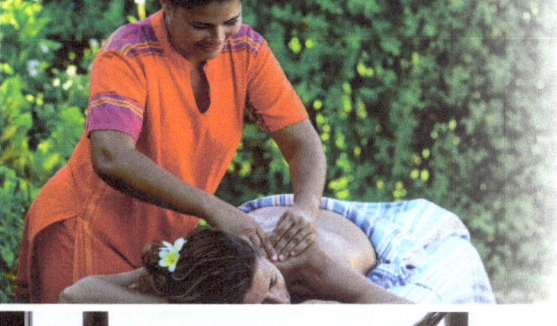

The Mozambique Collection

Small footprints, real people, exceptional experiences, amazing places ...

The Mozambique Collection is a marketing brand that brings together a collection of stunning properties working together to promote the destination. The hand picked portfolio of members each has it's own special attractions and experiences to contribute to the plethora of adventures that the country has to offer.

The underlying principle of authentic luxury, in the true sense, resonates with all members — to offer the best possible experiences in idyllic locations, while creating a positive legacy for the local communities and environment in which they operate.

www.mozambique-collection.org | info@mozambique-collection.org

EDITORIAL

ACCREDITATION

Official Travel Trade Journal and Media Partner to:

The Africa Travel Association (ATA)
Tel: +1 212 447 1357 • Email: info@africatravelassociation.org • Website: www.africatravelassociation.org

ATA is a division of the Corporate Council on Africa (CCA), and a registered non-profit trade association in the USA, with headquarters in Washington, DC and chapters around the world. ATA is dedicated to promoting travel and tourism to Africa and strengthening intra-Africa partnerships. Established in 1975, ATA provides services to both the public and private sectors of the industry.

The African Travel & Tourism Association (Atta)
Tel: +44 20 7937 4408 • Email: info@atta.travel • Website: www.atta.travel

Members in 22 African countries and 37 worldwide use Atta to: Network and collaborate with peers in African tourism; Grow their online presence with a branded profile; Ask and answer specialist questions and give advice; and Attend key industry events.

National Accommodation Association of South Africa (NAA-SA)
Tel: +2786 186 2272 • Fax: +2786 225 9858 • Website: www.naa-sa.co.za

The NAA-SA is a network of mainly smaller accommodation providers around South Africa – from B&Bs in country towns offering comfortable personal service to luxurious boutique city lodges with those extra special touches – you're sure to find a suitable place, and at the same time feel confident that your stay at an NAA-SA member's establishment will meet your requirements.

Regional Tourism Organisation of Southern Africa (RETOSA)
Tel: +2711 315 2420/1 • Fax: +2711 315 2422 • Website: www.retosa.co.za

RETOSA is a Southern African Development Community (SADC) institution responsible for tourism growth and development. RETOSA's aims are to increase tourist arrivals to the region through. RETOSA Member States are Angola, Botswana, DR Congo, Lesotho, Madagascar, Malawi, Mauritius, Mozambique, Namibia, Seychelles, South Africa, Swaziland, Tanzania, Zambia and Zimbabwe.

Southern Africa Tourism Services Association (SATSA)
Tel: +2786 127 2872 • Fax: +2711 886 755 • Website: www.satsa.com

SATSA is a credibility accreditation body representing the private sector of the inbound tourism industry. SATSA members are Bonded thus providing a financial guarantee against advance deposits held in the event of the involuntary liquidation. SATSA represents: Transport providers, Tour Operators, DMC's, Accommodation Suppliers, Tour Brokers, Adventure Tourism Providers, Business Tourism Providers and Allied Tourism Services providers.

Southern African Vehicle Rental and Leasing Association (SAVRALA)
Contact: manager@savrala.co.za • Website: w

Founded in the 1970's, SAVRALA is the representative voice of Southern Africa's vehicle rental, leasing and fleet management sector. Our members have a combined national footprint with more than 600 branches countrywide. SAVRALA are instrumental in steering industry standards and continuously strive to protect both their members' interests, and those of the public, and are therefore widely respected within corporate and government sectors.

Seychelles Hospitality & Tourism Association (SHTA)
Tel: +248 432 5560 • Fax: +248 422 5718 • Website: www.shta.sc

The Seychelles Hospitality and Tourism Association was created in 2002 when the Seychelles Hotel Association merged with the Seychelles Hotel and Guesthouse Association. SHTA's primary focus is to unite all Seychelles tourism industry stakeholders under one association in order to be better prepared to defend the interest of the industry and its sustainability as the pillar of the country's economy.

International Coalition of Tourism Partners (ICTP)
Website: www.tourismpartners.org

ICTP is a travel and tourism coalition of global destinations committed to Quality Services and Green Growth.

International Institute for Peace through Tourism
Website: www.iipt.org

IIPT is dedicated to fostering tourism initiatives that contribute to international understanding and cooperation.

World Travel Market
WTM Africa - Cape Town in April, WTM Latin America - São Paulo in April, and WTM - London in November. WTM is the place to do business.

World Youth Student and Educational (WYSE) Travel Confederation
Website: www.wysetc.org

WYSE is a global not-for-profit membership organisation.

The Safari Awards
Website: www.safariawards.com

Safari Award finalists are amongst the top 3% in Africa and the winners are unquestionably the best.

World Luxury Hotel Awards
Website: www.luxuryhotelawards.com

World Luxury Hotel Awards is an international company that provides award recognition to the best hotels from all over the world.

COVER STORY:

The April edition of the Tourism Tattler Trade Journal's front cover features the **Donkin Memorial**, which commemorates the city of Port Elizabeth and South Africa's colonial past. Erected by Rufane Shaw Donkin, who named the rising seaport of Algoa Bay as Port Elizabeth, the memorial was erected in memory of his wife in August 1820. The Hill Lighthouse next to the memorial pyramid was built in 1861.

Heritage and culture are key components to Nelson Mandela Bay (NMB) as a tourism destination, to such a degree that the NMB region (Port Elizabeth, Uitenhage, Despatch and Colchester) has been named after Nelson Mandela – humanitarian, freedom fighter and world icon of peace. Nelson Mandela Bay is the only geographical area which has been allowed to retain Madiba's name and possesses qualities that resonate with that of our beloved hero.

Locals from the friendly city openly invite you to "Experience the Spirit of Freedom" *(Ikhaya lenkululeko)* through the free smiles of their people, wide open beaches, endless wildlife viewing and an abundance of activities and attractions to be explored. With NMB being known as the City of Freedom, a person is able to experience the feeling of freedom through the stories and freedom routes fondly shared by locals.

Popular to explore is Route 67, which is a route that is depicted through 67 artworks symbolising Madiba's years dedicated to the freedom struggle. The 'Route 67' meanders through the CBD taking visitors past some of the Bay's oldest monuments, art deco architecture and a series of open-air artworks.

It is a destination where one enjoys the easy going lifestyle of NMB with a round of golf or a luxury spa treatment with cocktails at a 5 star facility. The climate is complementary to our breathtaking beaches where in summer the water temperature ranges from 18 to 21 degrees Celsius and in winter between 14 to 19 degrees Celsius allowing ideal opportunities for snorkelling, diving or surfing.

For the adventure seekers there are a variety of experiences to get the blood pumping. Adrenalin Addo is a family friendly attraction for anyone in pursuit of sheer fun and adventure and they are proud to lay claim to the longest double zip line in Africa and the only giant swing

of its kind in South Africa. Sandboarding is another must do activity that is a unique adventure that starts with a scenic boat cruise on the Sundays River where you will see the local birdlife feeding in their natural habitat. After about 10 minutes you reach the famous Alexandria Coastal Dune field which is the largest, most impressive and least degraded dune field in South Africa.

Due to its easy accessibility, Nelson Mandela Bay has become a popular tourist destination in its own right. NMB is a destination which is easily accessible by road, air, rail and sea travel. Popular among many visitors and locals is the "gift of time" as with little traffic congestion and the close proximity of attractions, accommodation facilities and restaurants, one can experience a multitude of activities in a short time frame. This is further enhanced by the Nelson Mandela Bay Pass card that, once purchased, allows free and discounted entry into a variety of attractions and activities *(read more on page 07)*.

Blue Flag status has been awarded to three beaches in NMB by the Wildlife and Environment Society of South Africa (WESSA) for the Blue Flag season of 2015/2016. These include Humewood, Hobie and Kings Beach.

Today South Africa is recognised as the producer of the highest quality mohair in the world. Mohair South Africa leads the global mohair market and Port Elizabeth renown as the Mohair Capital of the World. Over 60% of the world's mohair passes through the city. Take a tour at the Hinterveld factory in Uitenhage, a processing plant that is the epicentre of the world's mohair production.

While visiting the home of the Big 7 (Lion, Leopard, Cape Buffalo, Elephant, Rhinoceros, Southern Wright Whale and Great White Shark) be sure not to miss out on a wildlife experience at the nearby game reserves. Alternatively if good vibes and flavours are your style, we recommend a micro brewery tour, township buy and braai or a stroll through the Stanley Street restaurant area.

As a destination marketing body, Nelson Mandela Bay Tourism (NMBT) is honoured to introduce, and to be featured in, this month's edition of Tourism Tattler.

I encourage readers to experience the world-class quality service provided by our accommodation and activity establishments listed on pages 08 to 17. The commitment by NMBT members to promote and conserve a sustainable environment and community, while reducing waste and energy consumption in Port Elizabeth is a prime example of quality tourism services *(read more on page 20)*.

Moving on to my favourite subject, namely food, the feature stories on Organic Food for Conscious Conferencing *(page 24)*, African Cuisine *(page 28)*, and Food in Tourism Marketing *(page 32)* are of particular interest.

Yours in Tourism,

Mandlakazi Skefile
Guest Editor - Tourism Tattler

About April's Guest Editor

Mandlakazi Skefile is the Chief Executive Officer of Nelson Mandela Bay Tourism and is the woman responsible for bringing the world to Nelson Mandela Bay.

She has seen many successes during her term, including Port Elizabeth's hosting of the IRB World Series Sevens rugby tournament.

Born and bred here, Skefile says that her position is the perfect outlet for the passion she feels for the Bay. Her hobbies include spending time with her three children, travelling and cooking.

For more info visit www.nmbt.co.za

ATTRACTIONS

ATTRACTIONS

EXPLORE
Nelson Mandela Bay

Nelson Mandela Bay has become a rather popular destination with locals and visitors due to the accessibility and convenience to explore the city with the Nelson Mandela Bay (NMB) Pass Card.

Due to popularity and industry demand this has motivated Nelson Mandela Bay Tourism (NMBT) to create an electronic NMB Pass to further enhance the attractiveness of the destination.

The Nelson Mandela Bay Pass is a smartcard access card that provides tourists with free and discounted admission to a variety of attractions and activities in and around NMB. These include amongst others museums, game reserves, scuba diving, art galleries, sightseeing tours and many more. It also entitles the card holder to some great discounts in selected stores for shopping, activities, entertainment and more.

NMBT CEO, Ms Mandlakazi Skefile confirmed, *"NMBT has received various requests from tour operators and travel agents interested in selling the NMB Pass. Getting the physical cards to them was creating an obstacle in accessibility. Therefore after signing a deal with Thompsons to sell and promote the NMB Pass we decided to implement an additional card-less pass in the form of a voucher."*

Previously the NMB Pass would need to be purchased and collected in a card format to enable use. The process has however been simplified even further because it can now be emailed in a voucher format and works just like the physical NMB Pass card. To transact the e-pass one follows the same procedures as with the normal pass card. Additionally the voucher will also indicate exactly what type of pass it is, when it was purchased as well as when it will expire. This will make it easier to identify if the card is still valid or not.

Through the implementation of the upgrades NMBT is further enhancing the attractiveness of the destination aligned to international trends to be mobile friendly and eco-friendly thus enhancing the convenience and accessibility to explore Nelson Mandela Bay.

There are two types of Nelson Mandela Bay Visitors Passes (packages) namely the 5 in 1 pass as well as unlimited access passes. The unlimited pass rates start from as little as R200.00 for children and R300.00 for adults. The 5 in 1 NMB Pass costs R450.00 and R300.00 for children aged 3 – 12 years.

The 5 in 1 pass includes any five of the attractions and activities advertised and can be used on any day within the 3 month period. The card user also qualifies for the shopping and transport discounts available on the pass for the 3 month duration of the pass validity. The unlimited itinerary passes are valid for 1 day, 2 days, 3 days, and 7 days depending on the period purchased. The unlimited Pass cards are bought for a time frame and provide an unlimited amount of attractions to experience in the timeframe allocated.

For more information visit www.nmbt.co.za or www.nelsonmandelabaypass.co.za. Alternatively contact the TOURISM call centre on +27 (0)41 582 2575.

Photo Credit: Anje Rautenbach

ATTRACTIONS

Where to Stay in Nelson Mandela Bay

Accommodation in and around Port Elizabeth can be found on the **NMBT** website (www.nmbt.co.za/accommodation).

On the following pages are a few establishments that are listed on Tourism Tattler's Trade Directory, which has been categorised by location and experience.

Pine Lodge Resort

Driving south along Port Elizabeth's Marine Drive towards the Cape Recife Nature Reserve, an imposing sign beckons travellers to pop-in for a visit at **Pine Lodge Resort & Conference Centre**. So I did, and after a guided tour of the expansive facilities, I got to interview the resort's General Manager, Dale Tucker (**DT**).

The resort layout, facilities and range of activities are impressive - when and how did this all start?

DT: Pine Lodge actually started out as a caravan park in 1990 with a few caravan sites and an ablution block. Back then we pitched on the old Sea Acres Caravan Park site, but the Nelson Mandela Bay Municipality clearly had other plans as this is where The Boardwalk Hotel & Casino is now located, so we were offered this site next to the Cape Recife Reserve entrance gate, which turned out to be fortuitous as it's the perfect location for a seaside resort.

I don't see any pine trees around, so how did the name Pine Lodge come about?

DT: The owner, Dennis Tucker established Pine Lodge Resort in George with a few partners around 30 years ago, so when they expanded to Port Elizabeth the name was a logical extension as the same resort style concept of caravanning / camping with self-catering accommodation and on-site activities was planned from the outset. Dennis subsequently sold his interest in the George operation and now owns the PE operation outright.

It's certainly much more than a caravan park now - how many sites / rooms do you now have?

DT: We have 25 caravan and camping sites, all 4-star rated with electrical points, ablutions and scullery areas as well as a fully-equipped laundry, a childrens' play area, a games room, and a well stocked tuck shop. We also have 13 Site Cabins and 2 Cara-Cabins - a concept that is unique to Pine Lodge as these are built

The Hub Boutique Hotel

A Resort for all Reasons (and Seasons)

on caravan sites to combine the outdoor enjoyment of camping with the comfort of a fully equipped cabin, and available at an affordable price. Over time we then built 84 self-catering Luxury Chalets on sand dune elevated sites, each with its own private deck and braai area. Again, the Chalets are unique to Pine Lodge in that they have been built in pairs so that families can have an inter-leading door to the adjoining unit, and these are available in 4-, 6- and 8-sleeper configurations. For guests who prefer a Bed & Breakfast option, we also provide a full buffet-style English breakfast as well as a Continental option. Our on-site restaurant, 'Ziggy's' provides a venue for relaxing sundowners or quiet dinners overlooking the beach.

I noticed some zip-line platforms in the bush as I arrived - are activities a big part of the resort?

DT: Yes, the zip-line is operated by Base Camp Adventures who also offer a High Ropes Experience, Climbing Wall, Fatbike beach cycling tours, and Guided Walks. On-site activity facilities include a 9-hole mini-golf course, a trampoline, jungle gym, giant chess set, basketball court, Astro-turf court for 5-aside soccer, cricket and volleyball, a gymnasium and a fully-equipped games room with pool table, darts, table tennis and mini soccer. Our famous donkey cart rides take guests on a leisurely trip down to the Cape Recife lighthouse. There is also an on-site Spa for those looking for a little pampering. Then there are activities offered in the surrounding area, which include bird spotting in the Cape Recife Nature Reserve, the penguin colony at the SA Marine Rehabilitation & Education Centre, golf at the Humewood Golf Club, and game viewing in Nelson Mandela Metropolitan University's Grysbok Trail.

Then there's angling, scuba diving, snorkelling, surfing and kayak-fishing, which are also popular activities.

Leisure tourists are certainly well catered for - what about the business tourism side?

DT: Conferences, functions and weddings are a major part of our business, as are school excursion groups, and we have 7 venues that can cater for events ranging from 5 to 500 attendees or delegates. In fact Pine Lodge is one of the few venues in PE that can provide business conference and incentive groups with accommodation, catering and team-building activities - all onsite for up to 300 guests. We then also have an arrangement with other beachfront hotels for over-flow accommodation and provide a shuttle service, so in reality we can cater for much bigger conference groups and use their conference halls for break-away sessions.

Well, Pine Lodge Resort & Conference Centre certainly meets the needs of Port Elizabeth's leisure and business tourism sectors. To find out more visit www.pinelodge.co.za

The Hub Boutique Hotel, located in Port Elizabeth's business and leisure suburb of Walmer, offers 14 ultra-modern and stylish rooms with balcony or patio overlooking a tranquil garden and sparkling swimming pool.

This popular hotel provides free Wi-Fi throughout, and all rooms have a private bathroom, minibar, satellite TV (movies for the DVD player obtainable from the front desk), and tea and coffee making facilities.

The hotel's communal facilities include an open plan lounge area with ample seating and large flat-screen TV.

The dining area serves a daily breakfast or guests can enjoy drinks from the honesty bar.

The hotel also provides guests with a laundry and ironing service, a business centre, meeting and banqueting facilities, and an airport shuttle service (at a surcharge). Walmer Park Shopping Centre is 1 minute by car, while Port Elizabeth Airport is just 5 kilometres away.

For reservations contact The Hub on +27 (0)41 581 2127 or visit www.the-hub.co.za.

ATTRACTIONS

Where to Stay in
Nelson Mandela Bay

🔵 BEACH 🟢 BUSH 🔴 CITY

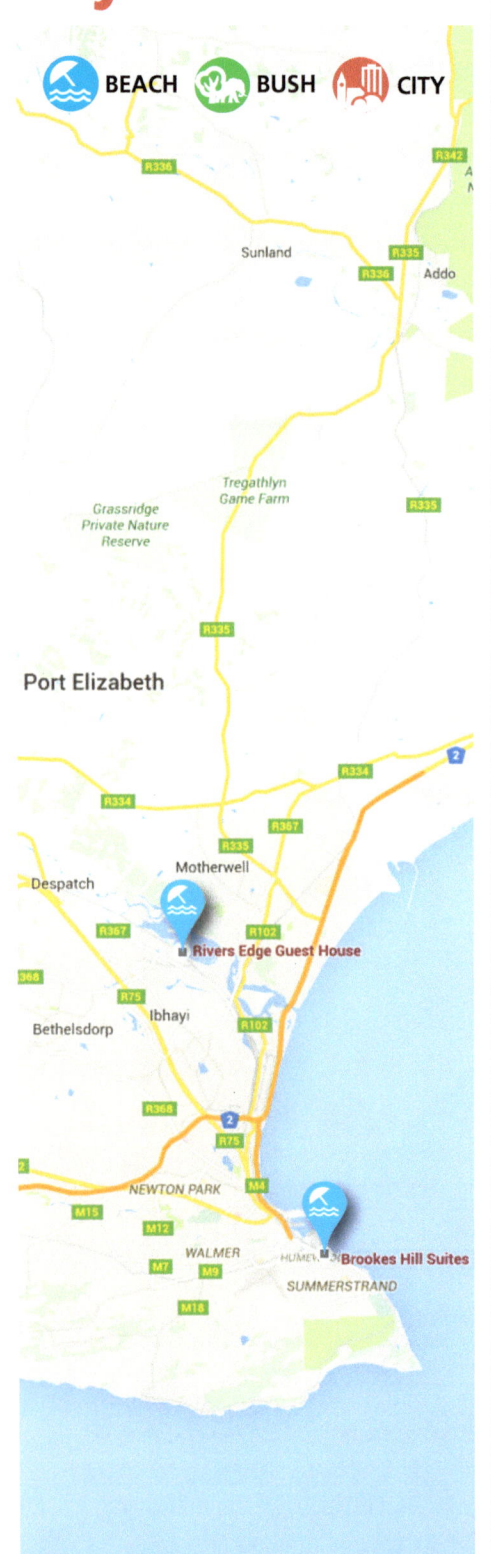

🏖️ Rivers Edge Guesthouse

Rivers Edge Guesthouse is an ideal home-away-from-home for corporate executives, leisure tourists and family holidays, in tranquil and natural surrounds, and right on the river's edge.

Located in Redhouse on the banks of Port Elizabeth's Swartkops River Estuary, the guesthouse overlooks the Zwartkops Wetland Conservancy and Aloes Nature Reserve.

With five en-suite rooms available, including a self catering garden cottage, Rivers Edge Guesthouse is only 15 minutes from either Port Elizabeth, Uitenhage or Despatch and an hour's drive to all world renown "Big 5" game parks in the malaria-free province of Eastern Cape. Day trips to the Addo Elephant Park, Shamwari Game Reserve and a host of other game parks are a mere 40 minutes away.

The village of Redhouse is a safe, friendly community that protects the interests of its residents and allows for both young families and older citizens to live active, healthy and neighbourly lives. Many activities in the village are organized for both visitors and villagers

🏖️ Brookes Hill Suites

Operated by Legacy Hotels & Resorts, **Brookes Hill Suites** is situated at the heart of Port Elizabeth's Beachfront.

Ideally positioned next to the Pavilion Complex restaurants, and overlooking the Happy Valley greenbelt, Brookes Hill Suites offers everything the leisure or business traveller could want, including PE's most popular beaches, shopping and entertainment centres, and the Oceanarium. A shuttle is also available for guests who want to visit the Boardwalk Casino & Entertainment World.

Hotel facilities include a salt-water pool overlooking the Indian Ocean with private

ATTRACTIONS

Birders Paradise on the river's edge

to mingle together, yet they also enjoy the private, quiet life that Redhouse has to offer.

The village offers a beautiful public garden, squash courts, lawn bowling green, yacht club, and rowing clubs. The University of Port Elizabeth (UPE) Rowing Club and the Grey High School Rowing Club are both based in Redhouse. Besides activities within Redhouse, there are also ample attractions and places of interest in and around the greater Port Elizabeth area to visit during your stay at Rivers Edge Guesthouse (read more here).

For mountain bikers, the Swartkops river estuary with its adjacent salt-pans that surround Rivers Edge Guesthouse provide a maze of interesting trails over flat terrain during the dry season.

For birders, the Swartkops Estuary is one of the best places in South Africa to see the less common estuarine waders, terns and greater flamingo. It is an important Bird Area, with over 10 000 waterbirds in summer and is one of the "must see" birding venues in Port Elizabeth.

For fishermen, casting a line from the private jetty in front of Rivers Edge Guesthouse can result in good catches, and saltwater fish species that can be hooked here include dusky kob, smallspotted grunter, white steenbras, Cape stumpnose, and Leerfish (aka Garrick). A series of surveys has accounted for 86 species of fish that commonly occur in the Swartkops river and estuary system.

For bookings call + 27 (0)72 224 9971 or email info@riversedge.co.za or visit www.riversedge.co.za

Everything the leisure or business traveller could want

access to the beachfront, a communal braai (barbecue) area set amid landscaped gardens, and ample parking space with 24 hour security.

Brookes Hill has 57 suites and studios, most of which have recently been refurbished to meet Legacy's exacting standards, and can

accommodate between 1 to 6 guests. There is also a rental pool of 100 self-catering (time share) suites available. Wireless connectivity is provided in all areas of the hotel.

For business meetings and functions, the Albatross conference venue offers conference facilities for up to 50 delegates and has

two breakaway rooms. The venue offers ample free parking, delightful garden lunch breakaways, and custom-made conference packages.

For more information call + 27 (0)41 584 0444 or email info@brookesexperience.co.za or visit www.legacyhotels.co.za

ATTRACTIONS

Where to Stay in
Nelson Mandela Bay & Surrounds

BEACH BUSH CITY

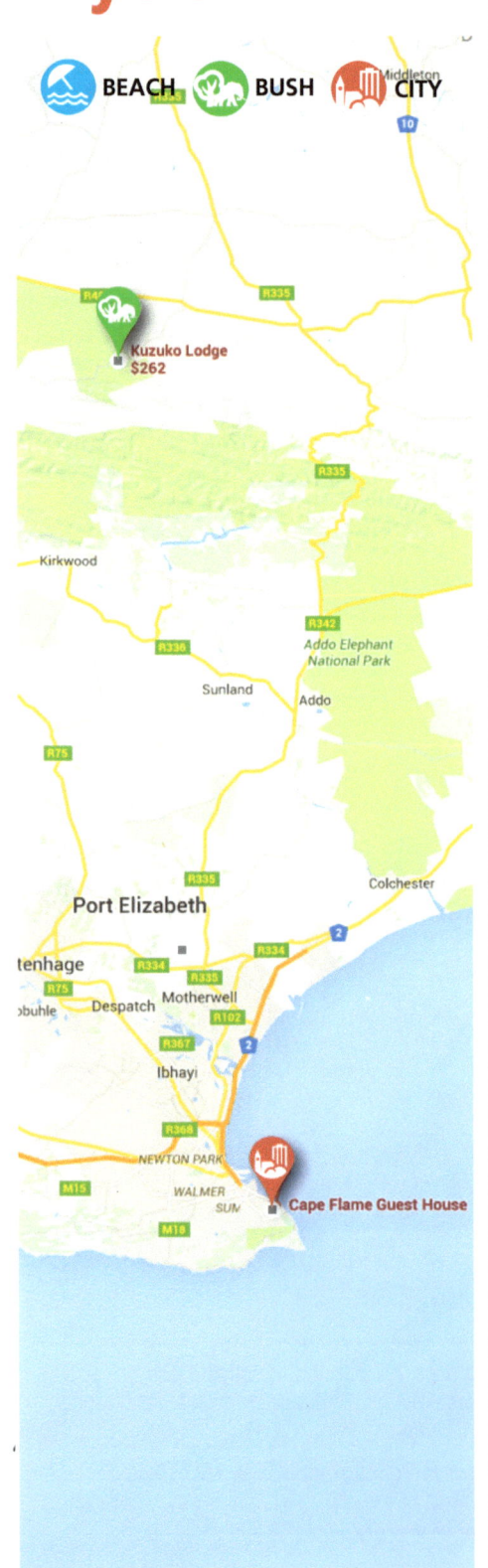

Cape Flame Guesthouse

The **Cape Flame** in Summerstrand, Port Elizabeth is best described as a stylish Boutique Hotel with the personal touch of a guesthouse. Only a stone's throw from Port Elizabeth's well-known Hobie Beach, Cape Flame offers TGCSA 4-Star-graded luxury accommodation.

Cape Flame offers corporate and leisure travellers both bed & breakfast and self-catering options. A delicious breakfast can be enjoyed in the stylishly appointed dining room, or in the tranquillity of the beautiful courtyard. Breakfasts include a'la carte and buffet options.

The hotel has eleven en-suite bedrooms, each uniquely decorated following a modern Africa theme reflecting the rich vibrancy of the continent. Bedrooms are equipped with a TV, mini bar, air conditioning unit and/or ceiling fans, and underfloor heating. There is also a complimentary tea and coffee service tray in the rooms.

Kuzuko Lodge

Operated by Legacy Hotels & Resorts, **Kuzuko Lodge & Reserve** is a private contractual area in the north of the greater Addo Elephant National Park – the third largest national park in South Africa in a malaria-free region.

With uninterrupted views of the Karoo Plains and the Zuurberg Mountains, Kuzuko Lodge is not only known as place of glory but also of absolute seclusion and tranquillity. This exclusive lodge is a must for every nature lover who enjoys to relax and take in the sounds of the wild.

Kuzuko means place of glory in the Xhosa native language. Once you stand on the restaurant deck upon arrival gazing over the never-ending expanse of the Karoo, you'll understand exactly why it's called *'Place of Glory'*. It's soul soothing…Think superbly appointed private chalets, sweeping hilltop

ATTRACTIONS

Hotel and Conference Centre

TV channels include DSTV satellite and MNet channels as well as other national channels.

While six of the rooms are situated in the main building, the other five rooms are located in the business retreat with added benefits for frequenting businessmen such as a mini-kitchenette and microwave oven.

Free WiFi is accessible throughout the property, which both businessmen and leisure guests will find convenient during their stay.

For conferences, meetings and functions, the stylish dining room can accommodate private functions for up to 25 in a group seating. This room also serves as a fully equipped conference room, able to comfortably seat 20 delegates in a "U" shape setting.

Cape Flame is close to restaurants, take-aways and a supermarket, while the beach and promenade is within walking distance.

For bookings call +27 (41) 583-3666 or visit www.capeflame.co.za

Place of Glory

vistas, sumptuous cuisine and a 'wilderness wellness centre' – The Main Lodge all perfectly integrated into the natural surrounds. Designed in such a way that the floor to ceiling windows ensure that the beauty of the location is never lost.

The deck, bar and restaurant offers stunning views while guest savour 5-star authentic Karoo Cuisine. The spacious family lounge offers free WiFi and space to spend quality time or simply snuggle up in front of the fire place. Guests can also visit our Curio shop for a memorabilia of their Kuzuko experience.

Guests are housed in 24 luxurious chalets, each with a private deck offering spectacular views of the malaria free big five reserve below. All chalets, of which three are wheelchair accessible, features an en-suite bathroom with bath and walk in shower, mini-bar, tea/coffee making facilities, colour television, telephones and free WiFi.

Chalets can either be made up as double or twin rooms with a sleeper coach for children under the age of 12. Kuzuko even offers kiddies friendly patio's to keep toddlers safe and secure without affecting the panoramic view.

For more information call +27 42 203 1700 or email *kuzuko@legacyhotels.co.za* or visit *www.legacyhotels.co.za*

ATTRACTIONS

What to Do & See in & Around NMB

UnTouched Adventures

Tsitsikamma National Park

The 2-3 hour Storms River Kayak & Lilo Adventure is **UnTouched Adventures'** most popular activity in Tsitsikamma National Park, located two hours (191.0 km) by car from Port Elizabeth via the N2 Garden Route.

Explore deeper into the Storms River Gorge, and experience the long, deep, quiet pools, and the majestic, pristine forests along the cliffs. We paddle from the Harbour next to the small beach, across the ocean, and then under the Suspension Bridge and up the beautiful Storms River Mouth.

If sea conditions don't allow for ocean paddling, we take a short guided hike through the Tsitsikamma Forest and start our kayak trip from inside the river mouth! We paddle right into the bats cave and spend time gazing up at the magnificent and spectacular cliffs all around us, all from the comfort of our double sit-on-top kayaks.

At the low-water point we disembark our kayaks and jump on our unique Lilo's *(a Lilo is an inflatable mattress that we've had specially made for this trip)*. From here we walk and float over a short section of rocks and simply wade deeper up the river on the Lilo's.

We also offer snorkelling in the tidal pools or along the Tsitsikamma underwater trails where you can marvel at the spectacular underwater world of the marine protected environment.

We are situated at the small boat harbour inside the Tsitsikamma National Park.

For bookings call +27 (0)73 1300 689 or email bookings@untouchedadventures.com or visit www.untouchedadventures.com

ATTRACTIONS

Stormsriver Adventures

Storms River Tsitsikamma

Stormsriver Adventures is based in Storms River Village in the heart of the Tsitsikamma National Park forest. All activities start at the adventure centre where one can choose between the world renowned Tsitsikamma Canopy Tours©, Tsitsikamma Woodcutters Journey and Guided Hikes & Team Building experiences.

Self catering accommodation is provided at The Green House, which is set in the heart of Storms River Village and is ideal for a family of four or two couples who want a special getaway treat.

Besides being Fair Trade and GreenLine certified, the company is the recipient of multiple awards for its support of local community projects, which include a school feeding scheme, animal welfare program, and HIV Aids awareness.

Founded in 1998, Stormsriver Adventures is one of the largest new job creators in the Eco Adventure industry in South Africa. Only local guides are employed with an emphasis on skills development.

Professional video and photos are included in the Canopy Tour experience, and to unwind from the adrenalin rush, visitors can relax at the Trees Restaurant, which is a job creation initiative that has capacitated ten local women from communities on the Garden Route. Or visit the Tsitsikamma Crafters who supply a range of locally produced crafts unique to the area.

For bookings call +27 (0)42 2811 836 or email adventure@gardenroute.co.za or visit www.stormsriver.com.

KAYAK & LILO ADVENTURE
CONTACT US
ua
UNTOUCHED ADVENTURES
Storms River Mouth
TSITSIKAMMA
+27(0) 73 1300 689
+27(0) 76 9592 817
BOOK NOW! www.untouchedadventures.com

KUZUKO LODGE
PLACE OF GLORY
Unlike any venue you have ever experienced
Known as the 'Place of Glory', Kuzuko Lodge is built high upon a hill in a private section of the Greater Addo Elephant National Park.
It is here, where breathtaking views from your private deck are complimented by luxurious chalets and warm, attentive service. This unique & glorious place is the perfect venue for either a Romantic Breakaway, Family Weekend, Teambuilding, Conference, Gala Event or Wedding.
www.kuzuko.com

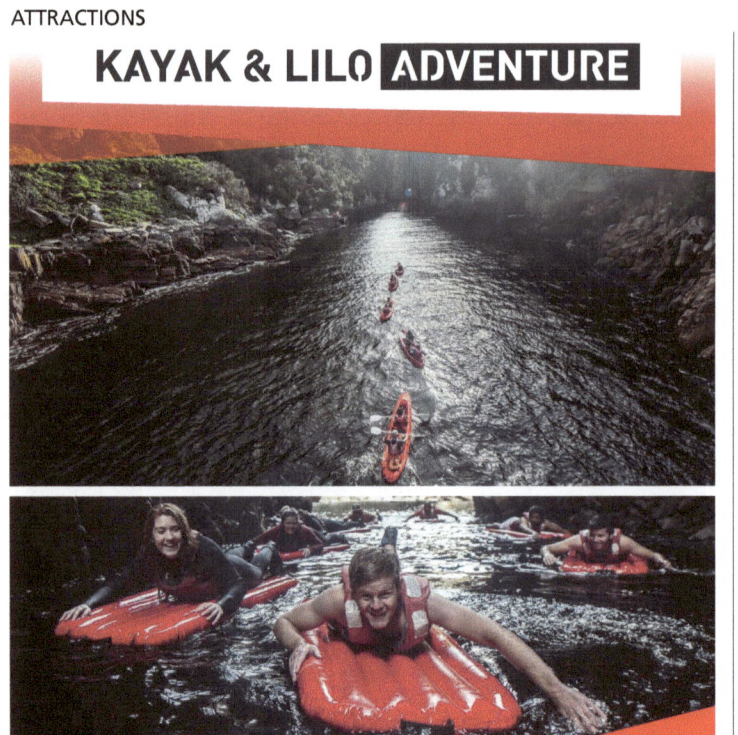

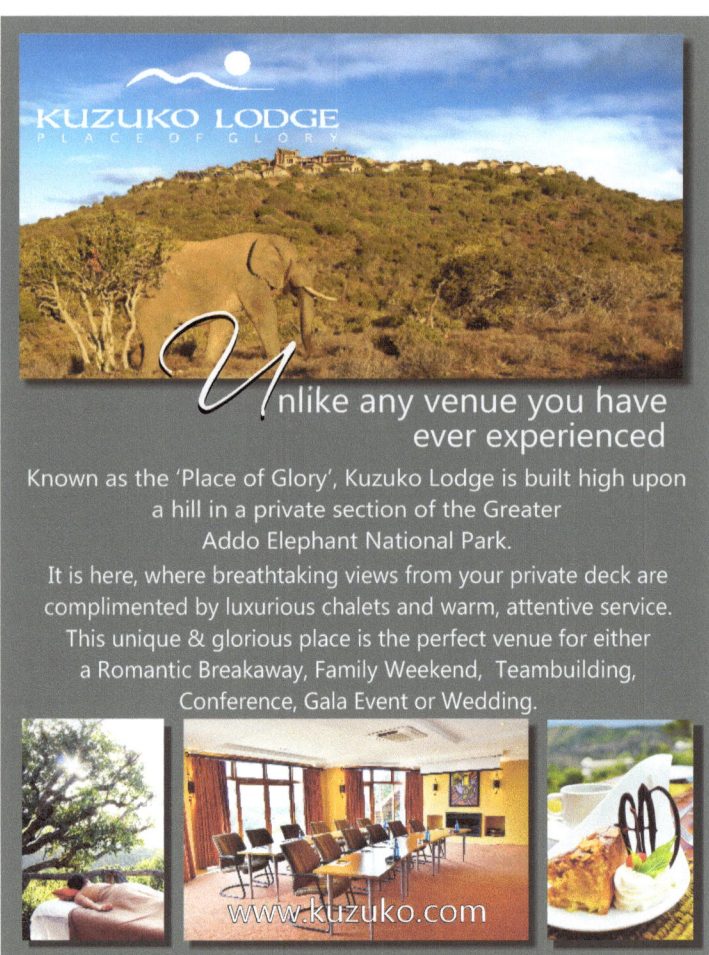

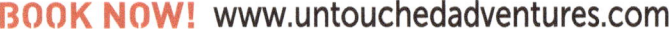

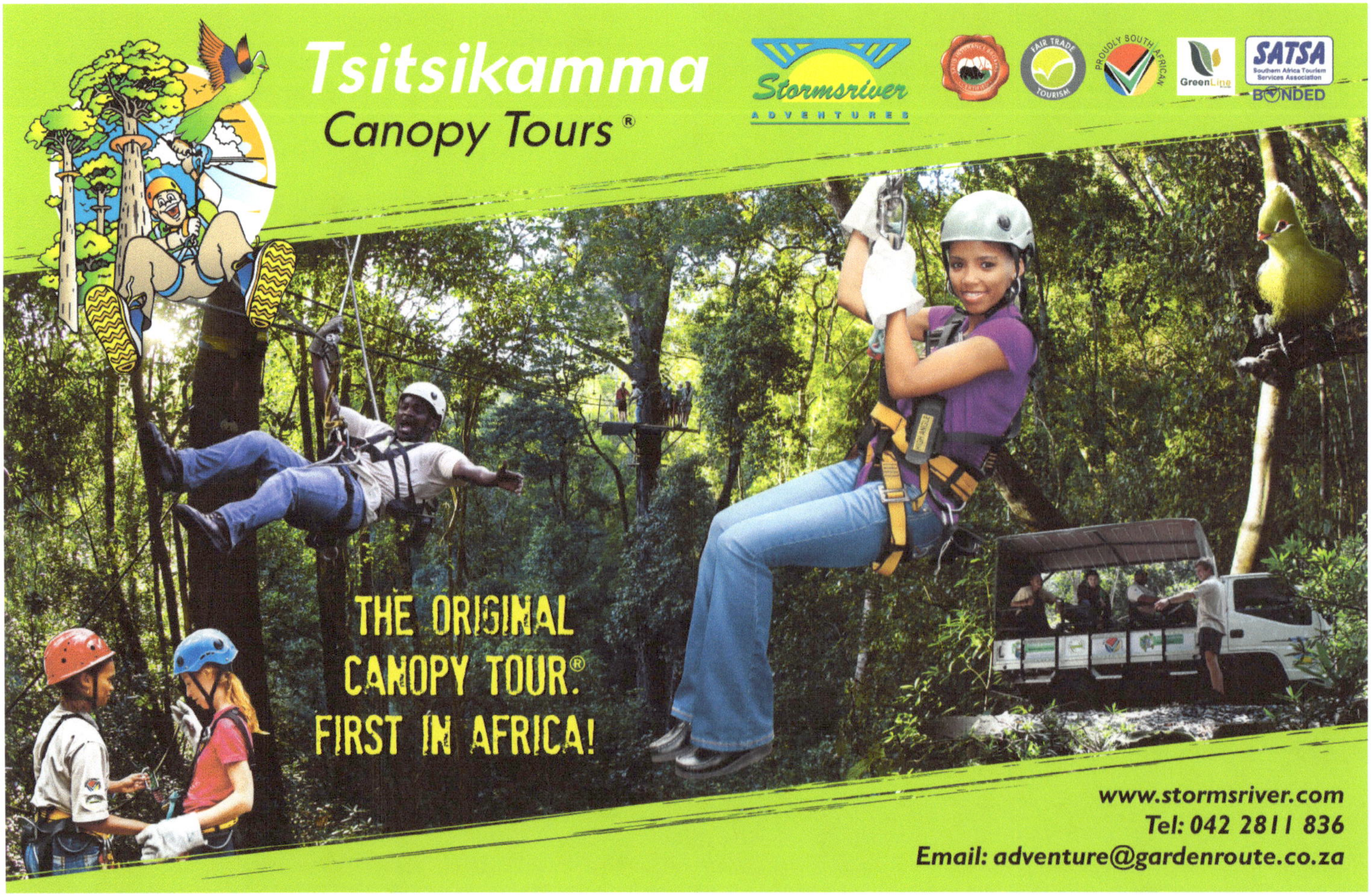
Tsitsikamma
Canopy Tours®
Stormsriver
ADVENTURES
FAIR TRADE TOURISM
PROUDLY SOUTH AFRICAN
GreenLine
SATSA
BONDED
THE ORIGINAL CANOPY TOUR® FIRST IN AFRICA!
www.stormsriver.com
Tel: 042 281 I 836
Email: adventure@gardenroute.co.za

ATTRACTIONS

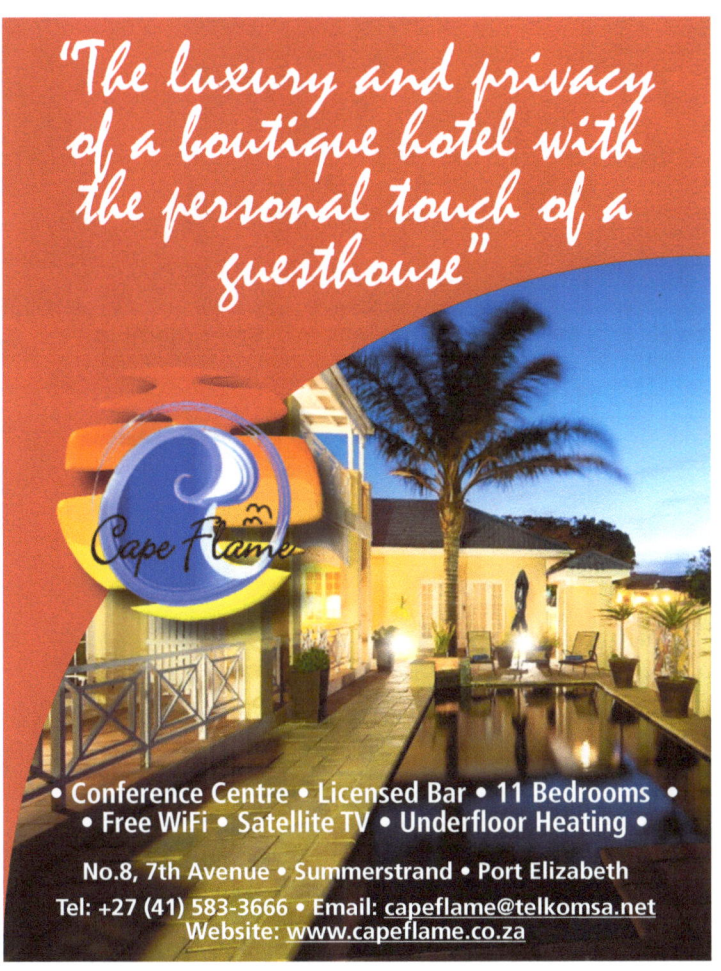

"The luxury and privacy of a boutique hotel with the personal touch of a guesthouse"

- Conference Centre • Licensed Bar • 11 Bedrooms
- Free WiFi • Satellite TV • Underfloor Heating

No.8, 7th Avenue • Summerstrand • Port Elizabeth
Tel: +27 (41) 583-3666 • Email: capeflame@telkomsa.net
Website: www.capeflame.co.za

WALMER - PORT ELIZABETH - SOUTH AFRICA

Experience a refreshing take on **corporate** & **leisure** accommodation...

THE HUB's modern furnishings, **EXCEPTIONAL VALUE FOR MONEY**, spacious rooms, **FREE WiFi** & central location make it the perfect destination when visiting Port Elizabeth.

THE HUB BOUTIQUE HOTEL ★★★

Tel: (041) 581-2127 • www.the-hub.co.za

Come and make a lifetime of memories in a single stay...

Imagine perfectly situated timber cabins merging with a coastal landscape. Imagine awaking to the sound of the ocean each morning. Imagine nature trails, spectacular scenery and nature's unspoilt beauty. Imagine Pine Lodge Resort & Conference Centre...

Minutes away from Port Elizabeth's main beachfront and Airport, Pine Lodge's log cabins are nestled amongst indigenous flora - only a stone's throw away from the ocean. The cabins are fully equipped for self-catering with private braai areas. A full buffet-style English breakfast is available and "Ziggy's" – the on-site restaurant – is open till late for relaxing sundowners or quiet dinners. The vast range of on-site activities including the 8m Highropes course, three ziplines and climbing wall as well as guided Fatbike Beach Tours and the River Spa all make for an unforgettable experience!

Come and experience our unique destination & make lifelong memories with us!

Tel: +27 (0)41 5834004
enquiries@pinelodge.co.za
www.pinelodge.co.za

★ ★ ★

BUSINESS & FINANCE

Market Intelligence Report

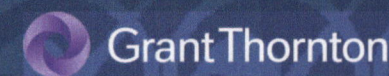

The information below was extracted from data available as at **29 March 2016**. By **Martin Jansen van Vuuren** of **Grant Thornton**.

ARRIVALS

The latest available data from **Statistics South Africa** is for **January to December 2015***:

	Current period	Change over same period last year
UK	407 486	1.4%
Germany	256 646	-6.5%
USA	297 226	-3.9%
India	78 385	-8.5%
China (incl Hong Kong)	84 878	2.2%
Overseas Arrivals	2 144 988	-4.9%
African Arrivals	6 746 114	-7.3%
Total Foreign Arrivals	8 903 773	-6.8%

HOTEL STATS

The latest available data from **STR Global** is for **January to December 2015**:

Current period	Average Room Occupancy (ARO)	Average Room Rate (ARR)	Revenue Per Available Room (RevPAR)
All Hotels in SA	63.4%	R 1 086	R 688
All 5-star hotels in SA	63.0%	R 1 981	R 1 249
All 4-star hotels in SA	62.6%	R 1 024	R 641
All 3-star hotels in SA	63.4%	R 871	R 552
Change over same period last year			
All Hotels in SA	1.4%	6.5%	8.0%
All 5-star hotels in SA	1.3%	9.5%	11.0%
All 4-star hotels in SA	2.2%	5.3%	7.6%
All 3-star hotels in SA	-0.2%	6.2%	5.9%

ACSA DATA

The latest available data from **ACSA** is for **February 2016**:

Change over same period last year	Passengers arriving on International Flights	Passengers arriving on Regional Flights	Passengers arriving on Domestic Flights
OR Tambo International	6.5%	6.2%	15.2%
Cape Town International	3.0%	38.1%	14.7%
King Shaka International	0.5%	N/A	14.3%

CAR RENTAL DATA

The latest available data from **SAVRALA** is for **January to June 2015**:

	Current period	Change over same period last year
Industry rental days	8 139 127	-1%
Industry utilisation	70.2%	-0.7%
Industry Average daily revenue	2 498 944 728	1%

WHAT THIS MEANS FOR MY BUSINESS

Analyses of Statistics South Africa data shows that foreign arrivals declined in 2015 and were at similar levels to 2013. A ray of hope is that foreign arrivals did start to increase in the last quarter of 2015. The ACSA data shows continued growth in passengers arriving on domestic flights. Passengers arriving on international flights have also started to increase.. *Note that African Arrivals plus Overseas Arrivals do not add to Total Foreign Arrivals due to the exclusion of unspecified arrivals, which could not be allocated to either African or Overseas. As from January 2014, Stats SA stopped counting people transiting through SA as tourists. As a result of the revision, in order to compare the 2015 figures with 2014, it has been necessary to deduct the transit figures from the 2014 totals.

For more information contact Martin at Grant Thornton on +27 (0)21 417 8838 or visit: http://www.gt.co.za

COMPETITION

The winning 'Like' or 'Share' during the month of **April 2016** will receive a **Dietz Monarch D10 Hurricane Lantern** with the compliments of **Livingstones Supply Co** – *Suppliers of the Finest Products to the Hospitality Industry*.

'Like' / 'Share' / 'Connect' with these Social Media icons to win!

Livingston Supply Company

Tourism Tattler

Competition Rules: Only one winner will be selected each month on a random selection draw basis. The prize winner will be notified via social media. The prize will be delivered by the sponsor to the winners postal address within South Africa. Should the winner reside outside of South Africa, delivery charges may be applicable. The prize may not be exchanged for cash.

Win

The **Dietz Monarch** was first introduced in 1900, and has been produced in at least seven distinct variations continuously over the past 108 years.

The first and oldest style Monarch had a flat top tank, un-reinforced air tubes, and a 9/16" fuel cap.

Congratulations to our March 2016 Social Media winner

Winner

🐦 **@Karoo_stories**

Chantelle the Tour Guide loves exploring the Karoo and Valley of Desolation in Graaff-Reinet South Africa. **Chantelle** will receive **two wildlife documentary DVD's by Derek and Beverly Joubert** with the compliments of **Livingstones Supply Co** – *Suppliers of the Finest Products to the Hospitality Industry*.

For more information visit www.livingstonessupplyco.com

ENVIRONMENT

CONSERVING ENERGY REDUCING WASTE

- Enviro Sustainability Case Study -

The Boardwalk Casino and Entertainment World in Port Elizabeth continues to subscribe by its mantra; reduce, reuse and recycle – a commitment to promote and conserve a sustainable environment and community, while reducing waste and energy consumption.

As captured in its environmental reports published since 2002, The Boardwalk has shown steady improvements in terms of its compliance with environmental standards in the leisure and tourism industry. Through its commitment to continually raising the bar in this regard, The Boardwalk and its tenants succeed in delivering a clean, environmentally-friendly and resource-efficient precinct. This ensures that visitors have the privilege of experiencing clean and well-maintained facilities, well-tended gardens, and healthy fish and other wildlife in the lakes.

Through Sun International's group-wide environmental initiative called SunGlow, The Boardwalk has set targets for the reduction of electricity usage by 5%, and waste sent to landfill by 3%.

"The Boardwalk has adopted the Sun International Group sustainability policy which provides the framework to which we operate in terms of environmental, social and corporate governance aspects. We have strict policies in place to ensure effective waste and water management. Everyone, at all levels, is encouraged to use resources sustainably, recycle where possible, and minimize waste.

"We are heartened by the progress we have made thus far. We have increased in the volumes of recycling collected and decreased the amount of waste to landfill, in line with our targets," says Peter Tshidi, Operations Manager at The Boardwalk.

The complex processes large volumes of waste, so to streamline the waste, the complex is divided into four distinct zones; the main casino zone, the hotel zone, the Magic Company, and the retail and restaurant zone.

Each of these four zones creates a constant flow of waste throughout the day. The zones also create their own particular type of waste and are served by dedicated waste yards.

Different bins are in use on the site to separate food waste from other types of waste such as wet waste, plastic, tin, metals and hazardous waste. Recyclables are safely bailed and transported to recyclers or to manufacturing companies for processing while organic waste is taken to a composting facility.

The Boardwalk aims to reduce the need to landfill and extract value from re-usable or recyclable material and even add value by making compost from organic waste.

The Boardwalk has a focused Environmental committee, with the Health and Safety Manager, Dean Blom, being the driving force behind The Boardwalk's Environmental Management System implementation. He ensures that environmental management receives constant attention.

Recognising that its employees have a fundamental role to play in ensuring the success and sustainability of its environmental sustainability initiatives, an awareness programme has been rolled out to educate them about saving electricity, conserving water and other issues around environmental responsibility.

"The Boardwalk's employees are trained on proper recycling processes and are encouraged to be ambassadors for the company's green ambitions. This includes adhering to environmental policies while at work and adopting green practices in their own homes.

"In everything we do, we strive to ensure that our business interests are harmonious with those of the environment. Our commitment to environmentally-sound business practices is strategic," concludes Tshidi.

Download The Boardwalk 2015 Environmental Report **here** *or visit the Boardwalk website at:* *www.suninternational.com/boardwalk/*

INKWENKWEZI
PRIVATE GAME RESERVE

Inkwenkwezi is situated in the malaria free Eastern Cape, only a 30 minute drive from East London at the start of the Wild Coast. Here one can view the magnificent Big Five or the other predators within the boundaries of the reserve.

We offer Game Viewing Safaris, Birding, Elephant Interaction Sessions, Elephant Walks, Quad Bike Tours, Walking Trails, Canoeing, Accommodation, Conferences and Weddings.

+27 (0)43 734 3234 / www.inkwenkwezi.com

pgr@inkwenkwezi.co.za

EVENTS

ASEAN NEWS

ASEAN TOURISM FORUM

ASEAN News Highlights:

- The Philippines laid out it's plan for a new international airport in Bohol (home to the unique 'chocolate hills'). The Panglao Airport is scheduled to open late 2017.

- Major renovations are ongoing at Singapore's Changi Airport, with a new airport terminal, nick-named Project Jewel, scheduled to open in 2018. The terminal will be five stories tall, showcase a spectacular indoor waterfall and increase the airport's passenger capacity to 24 million per year.

- A high speed railway link between Kuala Lumpur and Singapore is on the cards with construction expected to begin 2017 and completion scheduled for 2020.

- Thailand is seeking to promote experiences in the north and east of the country, taking guests beyond the already popular Bangkok and southern beaches.

- The *'free visit visa'* launched by Indonesia in 2015 saw international tourist arrivals increase by 19 percent.

- The Cruise south-east Asia brand was launched by the ASEAN Tourism Ministers on the last day of ATF. With tagline, *'Feel the warmth'*, it emphasises the warmth of south-east Asia's hospitality and references the region's year-round warm waters, which make it ideal for cruising.

TRADE EVENT REVIEW

2016 ASEAN Tourism Forum

By Tessa Buhrmann

The 2016 **Association of Southeast Asian Nations** (ASEAN) **Tourism Forum** (ATF) and the accompanying **TRAVEX** travel trade show, held in Manila recently, once again highlighted why this region is such a popular tourist destination. With experiences that range from extravagant luxury, wild and adventurous experiences to beaches and backpackers as well as the ever popular and growing niche of business and incentive travel, it's no wonder the ASEAN countries draw visitors from far and wide.

Philippines, the host of the 35th ATF, pulled out all the stops to make an impression on its 2,620 delegates comprising of ministerial and NTO delegates, as well as TRAVEX suppliers from across ASEAN, international buyers and media.

ATF TRAVEX featured a large and diverse collection of ASEAN suppliers, connecting in the region of 1,000 exhibitors with 457 buyers from around the world, alongside 175 international and local media.

The 3-day event running from 20-22 January incorporated close to 70 official sessions with the host country setting the bar high on several fronts – from the participation of 175 local exhibitors from across the Philippines, to a generous line-up of social activities including Pre-Show City Tours, the Opening Ceremony, Welcome Reception and Dinner, and Farewell Party for all ATF delegates, as well as other cocktail and exclusive dinner functions.

The Philippines certainly lived up to their slogan *'It's more fun in the Philippines'* with its wonderful Filipino hospitality, world-class infrastructure, facilities and services. A highlight for a number of international buyers and media was the opportunity of booking one of the Philippine Host Committee's ten post-ATF tours that ran from 23 to 26 January. This marked ATF's most extensive number of post-show tours in recent years. With a diverse range of itineraries including UNESCO sites and heritage tours, to islands hopping and highlands visits, proving that there is a Philippine destination to suit every taste.

The ATF is a co-operative initiative between the South-east Asian Nations to promote the ASEAN region as a single tourist destination. Member nations are: Brunei Darussalam, Cambodia, Laos PDR, Malaysia, Myanmar, Philippines, Singapore, Thailand and Vietnam. True to ATF's objectives of promoting the 10 ASEAN regions as a single destination, the spotlight at this year's event was not only on the Philippines. Other ASEAN NTOs displayed huge support and involvement in enhancing the 2016 ATF TRAVEX programme. In addition to their own showcase on the exhibition floor, Malaysia, Singapore, Thailand and Indonesia shared their own destination's appeal and hospitality, while evidencing ASEAN's strength of diversified experiences amidst a unified community during hosted lunches, late night functions and cocktail bashes.

The beauty of Southeast Asia most certainly lies in its warm and hospitable people, diverse culture, language and religion, its architecture, cuisine and geography – a blend of ancient and modern, where old centuries meet the 21st century. ASEAN captivates every spectrum of today's traveller – from adventure seekers, backpackers, businessmen, families to photography enthusiasts, those seeking sun, sand and sea, luxury and wellness as well as trekkers and wildlife enthusiasts.

The message from ATF2016 is that whether for business or for pleasure, Southeast Asia wants to continue maintaining a high level of tourist satisfaction, ensuring a meaningful experience to its tourists while raising their awareness about sustainability issues and promoting sustainable tourism practices amongst them.

Visit www.atf2017.com for more info.

About the author:

Tessa Buhrmann is the editor of **Responsible Traveller** magazine. She attended ATF2016 as a travel trade media correspondent on behalf of Tourism Tattler, and has written several interesting insights on Manila and the Phillipines from a responsible travellers perspective on her popular blog at www.responsibletraveller.co.za

EVENTS

Organic Food for Conscious Conferencing

As GMO (genetically modified organism) food concerns continue to be a top priority for the general public, the demand for organic food is growing, but are professional conference organisers taking advantage of this trend when planning catering needs for their delegates?

According to a 2015 Organic Industry Survey report by the Organic Trade Association, sales of organic food and non-food products in the United States broke through another record in 2014, totalling $39.1 billion, up 11.3 percent from the previous year. Organic sales now near a milestone 5 percent share of the total food market. The organic dairy sector posted an almost 11 percent jump in sales in 2014 to $5.46 billion, the biggest percentage increase for that category in six years.

In South Africa there are just 45 organic farms. One of these organic farms is located just outside Stellenbosch, on the Spier Wine Farm and it is from here that the Spier Conference Centre and restaurants on the estate source their wholesome food.

This organic farm operates as "Go Organic at Spier" and is a joint venture with seven emerging farmers, who together own 27.5% of the business. Spier used to lease 100 hectares of land from the local municipality, and this land is now used by the company and funded by the government's Land Reform Credit Facility. The farm is now one of South Africa's largest commercial organic farms, and is fully certified by Ecocert.

Managed by Angus McIntosh, Go Organic at Spier also retails its 'Pasture Reared Food' on his 'Farmer Angus' blog site.

According to 'Food with a Story', Angus uses the high density 'mobgrazing' technique for farming his grass fed cattle. Developed through observing the actions of herds of large wild herbivores, this method mimics nature and is particularly good at sinking carbon. "If ten percent of cattle in the world were grazed in this way, we wouldn't have the carbon issues we have today", says Angus.

Mobgrazing works by allowing the cattle to graze the top third of the grass plant (the healthiest bit) only before moving them along. The roots are then 'shed', effectively storing carbon in the soil. This allows for optimal grass growth, and carbon-negative beef.

At the Spier Farm, they also produce real free-range chickens and organic veggies. All the animals that are farmed for their meat are slaughtered on site. The slaughterhouse is about as good as a place like that gets – the staff are taught to respect the animals and revere and be humbled by the power that they have when taking an animal's life. *To be conscious.*

Angus hopes to raise awareness and erase consumer apathy about food production. "Agriculture causes the most destruction on the planet, but also presents the biggest opportunity to heal the planet, empower people and reduce poverty."

So do your conference delegates, and the planet, a favour by going organic when planning catering or selecting a conference venue.

Read more about Conscious Conferencing here or get Big Ideas for Small Meetings here, for Medium Meetings here, for Large Meetings here, and for Green Meetings here.

Contact the Spier Conference Team on +27 (0)809 1100 or visit www.spier.co.za or email conference@spier.co.za

EVENTS

HOSPITALITY

MOZAMBIQUE

PROPERTY PROFILE

HOSPITALITY

Travessia Beach Lodge
- The Mozambique Collection -

Located off the beaten track, with easy access from Inhambane airport or Vilanculos International airport, Travessia is an eco-beach lodge that is all about understated barefoot luxury.

The lodge is built on raised wooden decks with timber or roll-up canvas walls under a thatched roof. The four luxurious and secluded casa have 180° sea views. The lodge is entirely solar powered, ensuring a light environmental foot print.

Take a walk on the endless beach, relax in the shade of the palm grove, paddle out or gaze at the sea from the rim-flow pool or accept an invite from the neighbouring community. Sophisticated whilst down to earth, with no one around for miles, Travessia is for families, individual travellers and couples alike.

"The Mozambique Collection is all about collaboration in promoting Mozambique as an international tourist destination, and we feel that the uniqueness of Travessia Beach Lodge, will contribute more depth and variety to the collection of properties, which already include Nkwichi Lodge, Ibo Island Lodge, Nuarro Lodge and Bahia Mar Boutique Hotel", says Kim Rossi, manager of The Mozambique Collection.

Travessia Beach Lodge is nestled between coastal forest and palm trees on the dunes along an endless beach. At low tide, the surf is perfect to take the canoe for a paddle and both children and adults will enjoy boogie boarding whilst the little ones love the small natural "pools" that are created when the tide goes out. There are no hawkers trying to sell you local curios. Depending on the weather offshore, you will find plenty of different shells and bleached coral on your beach walk. The Travessia team keeps their beach clean by regularly collecting all waste that gets washed up on the beach a few hundred meters up and down the property.

The Restaurant menu is inspired by what is in season and available at the local markets and shops. Fresh fish and crayfish are sourced from the local spear-fishermen. Whilst mango, pawpaw or avocado are seasonal, coconuts are available all year round.

A short walk from the restaurant leads to the beach bar and rim-flow plunge pool. Here, guests can stretch out on locally made loungers whilst enjoying 360 degree views over the endless coastline and a sea of palm trees towards the hinterland.

Early afternoon braais on the pool deck with drinks from the bar, which is well stocked with local beers, soft drinks, a selection of South African wines and spirits, provide a perfect setting for viewing sun-sets over the warm Indian ocean.

It's no wonder that guests have rated Travessia Beach Lodge 10/10 on TripAdvisor.

For more information visit travessialodge.com

About The Mozambique Collection

The Mozambique Collection showcases some of the most exciting, unique and intimate destinations, accentuating the variety found in Mozambique, one of Africa's most incomparable, rapidly developing and beautiful country.

The brand brings together a collection of stunning properties working together to promote the destination. The hand picked portfolio of members each has it's own special attractions and experiences to contribute to the plethora of adventures that the country has to offer.

The underlying principle of authentic luxury, in the true sense, resonates with all members – to offer the best possible experiences in idyllic locations, while creating a positive legacy for the local communities and environment in which they operate.

For more information visit www.mozambique-collection.org

HOSPITALITY

African Cuisine

By **Bennet Otoo**

According to Abraham Maslow's theory of needs, food is one of the very basic necessities of life. So basic that inadequate intake or a complete absence of food causes various health problems or in extreme cases, death. It is so central to life that, regardless of where you are in the world, there is a good meal that is peculiar to that locality.

In Africa, just like the various cultures, food is also prepared differently with many different ingredients. Every country or tribe has it's own tasty food which is peculiar to that country or city.

In Ghana, the more common food joints are small local meal hubs known as "chop bars" which can be found in every corner of the country.

With globalization and many Ghanaians spread all over the world, chop bars are now found in major cities such as New York and London.

Waakye

Waakye is a combination of **rice and beans**, which is both delicious and nutritious.

Usually served for breakfast or lunch with a typical spicy Ghanaian pepper sauce.

Ghana

Thieboudienn

Thieboudienn is a traditional Senegal dish made from **fish, rice, tomato sauce** and **vegetables**.

The name of the dish is derived from Wolof words meaning 'rice' and 'fish'.

Senegal

Images and text provided courtesy of **Jovago.com** - Africa's #1 online hotel booking portal.

HOSPITALITY

The Ndole

The Ndole is like the Cameroonian flag; revered by children and worshiped by the elders.

The Ndole is a mixture of **spinach, fresh peanut paste, crayfish, shrimp** and **beef** preferably with bones.

🇨🇲 Cameroon

Ofada rice

Ofada rice is a specially made delicacy with a unique aroma and original flavour. Its rich brown colouring and exotic taste makes it a family favourite across the country.
Usually accompanied with **goat sauce** and **plantain**, it's a perfect combination of sweet and spicy!

🇳🇬 Nigeria

Nyama Choma

Nyama choma means 'barbecued meat' in Kiswahili.
It is always eaten with the hands, and common side dishes include **kachumbari** (tomato and onion) salad and **ugali** (maize, millet, or Sorghum flour).

🇰🇪 Kenya

Images and text provided courtesy of **Jovago.com** - Africa's #1 online hotel booking portal.

HOSPITALITY

Rolex

The 'Rolex' has nothing to do with watches. It's a favourite anytime snack or light meal in Uganda.

Its name is derived from the saying "**roll of eggs**". It might be compared to a **breakfast-burrito** or **rolled omelette**.

Uganda

Injera with Doro

Doro is a thick spicy stew served with boiled eggs and is a local delicacy in Ethiopia. It's served with **injera** (fermented teff flour). The stew is piled on top of the bread, thus allowing the injera to soak up the juices, which creates a unique combination.

Ethiopia

Garba

Garba is the slang name for **Attiéké** (cassava). It is a popular dish made from Ivorian **manioc** (the starchy cassava or Yuca tuber), which is sold in small street stalls usually held by men. It consists of Attiéké in a couscous shape and pieces of fried salted tuna.

Ivory Coast

Images and text provided courtesy of **Jovago.com** - Africa's #1 online hotel booking portal.

HOSPITALITY

Chips Mayai

Chips Mayai is one of the most widely available and popular Tanzanian street foods in the country.

It consists of French fries and eggs, or to put it more accurately, a **French fries omelette**.

Tanzania

Couscous

Couscous is a North African dish made of semolina and is traditionally served with various meats and vegetables.

Algeria

Cachupa Rica

Cachupa Rice is a famous dish from the Cape Verde or Cabo Verde islands. It's a slow cooked stew of **corn, beans, cassava, sweet potato, fish** or **meat**. Each island has its own regional variation.

Cap Verde

Images and text provided courtesy of Jovago.com - Africa's #1 online hotel booking portal.

LEGAL

The Consumer Protection Act

CANCELLATION, PENALTIES & NON-REFUNDABLE DEPOSITS

- Part 3 - FINAL

SECTION 48: UNFAIR, UNREASONABLE OR UNJUST CONTRACT TERMS

This section not only addresses the contract terms but also the sales process ('the manner') and the waiver of rights and assuming of obligations – if we consider these in the broadest conservative terms, I believe it includes the issue under discussion.

As with section 41, this section contains a deeming provision *[Section 48 (2) and read with regulation 45]* and any of the aforesaid will be deemed to be *'unfair, unreasonable or unjust'* if it is *'excessively one-sided, inequitable or the presentation is false or misleading'*.

So, how does a supplier deal with it to ensure he/she does not fall foul of this section? Clearly the non-refundable deposit can be seen to be 'one-sided' but I don't be believe it is 'excessively' so as to be 'inequitable' provided it meets the norms prescribed in section 17 and are carefully explained and, as one travel agent does, the explanation is detailed in a separate sheet signed by the client.

SECTION 49: NOTICE REQUIRED FOR CERTAIN TERMS AND CONDITIONS

WHAT: This section *[Section 49 (1) & (2)*]* requires certain aspects of the transactions to be brought to the specific attention of the consumer and such aspects include the following, which I believe includes the topic under discussion:
(a) limit in any way the risk or liability of the supplier or any other person;
(b) constitute an assumption of risk or liability by the consumer.
* presence of which the consumer could not reasonably be expected to be aware.

HOW: It must be in writing, *'conspicuous'* and of such a nature that it will *'attract the attention of an ordinarily alert consumer'*.

WHEN: It must be drawn to the attention of the consumer at the earliest of when the contract is entered into or payment is made.

It is important to note that is can't be done at the last minute ('by the way') or in a rush as must be done in such a way that the consumer *[per Section 49 (5)]* has an *'adequate opportunity in the circumstances to receive and comprehend the provision or notice'*.

THE CONSEQUENCES OF NON-COMPLIANCE/BREACHING PROVISIONS

'A' SECTION 51: PROHIBITED TRANSACTIONS, AGREEMENTS, TERMS OR CONDITIONS

Any transgression of any of the above will result in such activity being void and thus unenforceable *[Section 51 (3)]* - it could mean the section/clause or the entire agreement!

'B' SECTION 52: POWERS OF COURT TO ENSURE FAIR AND JUST CONDUCT, TERMS AND CONDITIONS

This section pertains to a transgression of sections 40, 41 & 49.

Factors the court must consider:
- Did the consumer get fair value?
- The balance of power. e.g. knowledge & literacy of consumer such as first time traveler.
- Forseeable circumstances.
- Conduct of the parties.
- Use of plain language.

Section 52 (2) (h) – important for T&C and record-keeping:
- Whether the consumer knew or ought reasonably to have known of the existence and extent of any particular provision of the agreement that is alleged to have been unfair, unreasonable or unjust, having regard to any:
(i) custom of trade; and
(ii) any previous dealings between the parties.
- Steps the court may take:
  (i) Court determines transaction or agreement was, in whole or in part, unconscionable, unjust, unreasonable or unfair *(i.e. sections 40 & 48)* – order supplier to:
    (i) Restore money or property to the consumer;
    (ii) Compensate the consumer for losses or expenses relating to:
      (aa) the transaction or agreement; or
      (bb) the proceedings of the court;
    (iii) Require the supplier to cease any practice, or alter any practice, form or document, as required to avoid a repetition of the supplier's conduct.
- Person alleges that an agreement, a term or condition of an agreement, or a notice to which a transaction or agreement is purportedly subject, is void in terms of this Act *(Section 51)* or failed to satisfy any applicable requirements set out in section 49;
- If void: sever part of the agreement, provision or notice; alter it; declare the entire agreement, provision or notice void retroactively;
- If breaching section 49: sever the provision or notice from the agreement; declare it to have no force or effect;
- IN ADDITION to the above it can 'make any order that is just and reasonable'.

'C' SECTION 100: COMPLIANCE NOTICE & PENALTIES

- The consumer commissioner ('CC') can issue a compliance notice i.e. requiring supplier to rectify transgression;
- Failing that the CC can impose penalties.

'D' SECTION 111: PENALTIES (if convicted of offence)

- Contravention of section 107 (1) (Breach of confidence), to a fine or to imprisonment for a period not exceeding 10 years, or to both a fine and imprisonment; or
- in any other case, to a fine or to imprisonment for a period not exceeding 12 months, or to both a fine and imprisonment.

'E' SECTION 112: ADMINISTRATIVE FINES (National Consumer Tribunal)

An administrative fine imposed in terms of this Act may not exceed the greater of 10 per cent of the respondent's annual turnover during the preceding financial year or R1 000 000.

When determining an appropriate administrative fine, the Tribunal must consider the following factors:
- The nature, duration, gravity and extent of the contravention;
- any loss or damage suffered as a result of the contravention;
- the behaviour of the respondent;
- the market circumstances in which the contravention took place;
- the level of profit derived from the contravention;
- the degree to which the respondent has co-operated with the Commission and the Tribunal; and
- whether the respondent has previously been found in contravention of this Act.

NOTE: The Risk in Tourism series (The Law: Contracts) will continue with Part 18 in the May 2016 edition.

Disclaimer: *This article is intended to provide a brief overview of legal matters pertaining to the travel and tourism industry and is not intended as legal advice. © Adv Louis Nel, 'Louis The Lawyer', April 2016.*

MARKETING

FOOD
in Tourism Marketing

By **Dr. Peter E. Tarlow**

There is little doubt that food is a major part of the tourism experience. Because eating is an essential part of living, food or culinary tourism has a broad base of appeal. In fact, often when visitors return home, one of the first questions that people ask is *"how is the food?"*

The interaction between tourism and food is often called culinary tourism. In reality this is a broad term that often means different things to different people. Scholars define culinary tourism along the lines of: *visitors having the opportunity of partaking in unique and memorable eating and drinking experiences*. Culinary tourism tries to provide authentic local cuisines that represent both the tastes and smells of a nation as a part of that locale's cultural offerings and heritage. This definition, however, may speak more to a locale's *'haute cuisine'* than to the eating experience of the average local resident.

The World Food Tourism Association supports this assertion, noting that *"only 8.1% of all foodies self-identify with the 'gourmet' label."* Thus the association argues that most people enjoy good food and drink but there is no necessary relationship between the enjoyment of a culinary experiences and the cost of that experience.

Often the most interesting culinary experiences come from a variety of social and economic classes. Furthermore, every community has a culinary food potential, although often visitors or tourists do not get to experience it and at times the local population under appreciates it.

For some ideas, cautions, and experiences aimed at helping you create a local culinary tourism experience that will add pride to your own community, simply subscribe to my latest Tidbits newsletter at:
www.tourismandmore.com/tidbits-newsletter-signup/

About the Author: Dr. Peter E. Tarlow publishes a monthly 'Tourism Tidbits' newsletter. He is a founder of the Texas chapter of TTRA, President of T&M, and a popular author and speaker on tourism. Tarlow is a specialist in the areas of sociology of tourism, economic development, tourism safety and security. Tarlow speaks at governors' and state conferences on tourism and conducts seminars throughout the world. For more information e-mail ptarlow@tourismandmore.com

RISK

UNDERSTANDING Tourism Trade Insurance

- Part 4 -

Part 1 in this series covered an introduction to insurance, an outline on the EC Directive, the basics of risk management, and financial guarantees. Parts 2 and 3 looked at liability insurance, while Part 4 continues the subject of liability with specific reference to the Road Accident Fund in South Africa.

ROAD ACCIDENT FUND - SOUTH AFRICA

What is the Road Accident Fund?
The Road Accident Fund is a public entity, which has been set up to pay compensation to people injured in road accidents or the dependants of people killed in road accidents arising from the negligent driving of a motor vehicle in South Africa.

Where does the Fund get its money from?
The Fund gets its money from a fuel levy included in the price of petrol and diesel, which is paid by drivers of motor vehicles.

Is a lawyer required?
The Fund employs staff at all regional offices and at various public hospitals to assist claimants free of charge. However a claimant may still decide to employ a lawyer. The lawyer will be entitled to charge a fee for professional services rendered.

Time period to make a claim
If the identity of the offending driver or owner is known, the claim must be lodged within three years from the date on which the claim arose. (This does not apply to a claim of a minor). If the identity of the offending driver or owner is unknown, the claim must be lodged within two years from the date on which the claim arose.

Who is entitled to make a claim?
1. A person who was personally injured (except a driver who was the sole cause of the accident).
2. A dependant of a deceased victim.
3. A close relative of the deceased in respect of funeral expenses.
4. A claimant under the age of 18 years must be assisted by a parent or legal guardian.

What can you claim for?
- Medical expenses (past and future);
- Funeral expenses;
- Loss of earnings or income if person is disabled (past and future);
- Loss of support for a dependant of a deceased victim (past and future)
- General damages for pain, suffering and disfigurement in the case of bodily injury. Note: (This is determined after examining the extent and severity of the injury).

TYPES OF INSURANCE
The five kinds of insurance that apply to the tourism industry:
1. Financial Guarantee (Insurance Bond) - *Refer January issue*.
2. Liability Insurance
3. Vehicle / Property Insurance
4. Travel Insurance / Medical Rescue
5. Other Business Insurance (Buy & Sell, Key Person, Provident Fund)

How is a claim made against the Fund?
- A claim must be made on the Claim Form, *(Form 1 is to be used in respect of claims arising prior to 01 August 2008, and RAF1 for 01 August 2008 onwards)* which is available from offices of the Road Accident Fund.
- Every applicable paragraph must be fully completed.
- The doctor that treated the injured person immediately after the accident must complete the medical report section in the claim form.
- The claim form must be signed by the claimant.

What documents must be submitted with the claim form?
In the case of injury the following documents must be attached:
1. A certified copy of the identity document of the claimant;
2. An affidavit by the claimant;
3. The Police report (OAR), police statements and police sketch plan;
4. Documents to prove loss of earnings e.g. salary advice slip;
5. Documents to prove medical expenses;
6. Copies of hospital records if available;
7. A serious injury assessment report (in respect of claims arising after the 31 July 2008) where general damages are claimed.

If the accident victim is deceased the following additional documents are required:
8. Identity document of deceased;
9. Death certificate or post-mortem report;
10. Documentary proof of marriage (if claim by spouse);
11. Full unabridged birth certificates reflecting the names of parents;
12. Proof of earnings of all parties involved;
13. Proof of reasonable funeral expenses.

The claim form and the accompanying documents must be hand delivered or sent by registered mail to the Fund at the addresses appearing under the Contact Details at www.raf.co.za

Important considerations:
- Property damage cannot be claimed from the Fund, it may be claimed from the offending driver;
- An accident must be reported to the police and the Fund by the driver/owner;
- Compensation will be reduced in relation to claimant's own negligence;
- Compensation for a passenger in the offending vehicle is limited to R25 000 in respect of claims arising prior to 01 August 2008.
- Compensation received from the Compensation Commissioner in a case where a person is injured on duty, is deductible.
- The Fund may require a person to submit to investigations and medical examinations;
- A claim may be excluded in a case where a claimant unreasonably refuses or fails to cooperate with the Fund in the course of its investigation.
- There are certain categories of claims that the Road Accident Fund Act excludes.

The Road Accident Fund Amendment Act, No19 of 2005, which came into effect on the 1 August 2008 brought about the following changes to claims arising after 31 July 2008:
- The limit of R25 000.00 placed on the claim of a passenger in the offending vehicle, has been removed.
- General damages claims are subject to an assessment by a registered medical practitioner, to determine the severity of the injuries suffered and whether or not the injury is to be classified as a "serious injury "
- Damages for loss of support are capped at R219 820.00 (as at 30 April 2014) per year in respect of each deceased breadwinner.
- Damages for loss income are capped is capped at R219 820.00 (as at 30 April 2014) per year.
- The maximum amount upon which claims for loss of income and loss of support are calculated (R219 820.00) is subject to an annual inflationary adjustment in line with the official CPI measure.
- Emergency medical treatment costs are payable by the Fund in accordance with a prescribed tariffs. (NHRPL tariff)
- Non-Emergency medical treatment costs are payable by the Fund in accordance with the Uniform Patient Fee Schedule for full paying patients
- The exclusion of claims by members of the same household as the driver of the motor vehicle has been removed, and such claims are now permissible.
- The exclusion of claims by fare-paying motorcycle passengers has been removed, and such claims are now permissible.

It is important to note the effect that the Road Accident Fund legislation has on the tourism industry in terms of legal action following a motor vehicle accident. The abolition of the injured party's (passenger / tourist / guest) common law right to sue the wrongdoer (operator), means that following a motor vehicle accident the severely injured tourist will only receive limited compensation from the Road Accident Fund and will have no right of recourse against the wrongdoer.

As South Africa's primary inbound markets emanate from European Union countries and are subject to the E.C. Directive on Travel and Trade Act, agents will find themselves even more exposed to risk. If an injured guest's damages cannot be recovered against the local operator, their client will no doubt seek to hold them responsible in terms of said directive.

This article will be be continued in the May 2016 edition of the Tourism Tattler, and will explain **Personal Accident** *and* **Professional Indemnity** *insurance - Ed.*

Get the Tourism Insurance Directive booklet

DOWNLOAD (PDF - 4.4MB)
www.tourismtattler.co.za/downloads/SATSA-Insurance-Directive-2015-Digital.pdf

PRINTED COPY
Collect at SATSA's offices: 3rd Floor, Petrob House, 343 Surrey Avenue, Ferndale, Johannesburg
or email communications@satsa.co.za (Note that a nominal fee will be charged for admin, postage or courier costs)

www.ingramcontent.com/pod-product-compliance
Lightning Source LLC
Chambersburg PA
CBHW050410180526
45159CB00005B/2215